D1567685

STONEHENGE

BY LISA OWINGS

EPIC

BELLWETHER MEDIA · MINNEAPOLIS, MN

EPIC BOOKS are no ordinary books. They burst with intense action, high-speed heroics, and shadows of the unknown. Are you ready for an Epic adventure?

This edition first published in 2015 by Bellwether Media, Inc.

No part of this publication may be reproduced in whole or in part without written permission of the publisher. For information regarding permission, write to Bellwether Media, Inc., Attention: Permissions Department, 5357 Penn Avenue South, Minneapolis, MN 55419.

Library of Congress Cataloging-in-Publication Data

Owings, Lisa.
  Stonehenge / by Lisa Owings.
    pages cm. – (Epic: Unexplained Mysteries)
  Includes bibliographical references and index.
  Summary: "Engaging images accompany information about Stonehenge. The combination of high-interest subject matter and light text is intended for students in grades 2 through 7"– Provided by publisher.
  Audience: Ages 7-12.
  ISBN 978-1-62617-204-3 (hardcover : alk. paper)
  1. Stonehenge (England)–Juvenile literature. 2. England–Antiquities–Juvenile literature. 3. Megalithic monuments–England–Juvenile literature. I. Title.
  DA142.O85 2015
  936.2'319–dc23
                              2014041513

Designed by Jon Eppard.

Printed in the United States of America, North Mankato, MN.

TABLE OF CONTENTS

A SACRED CIRCLE

A crowd gathers on an English field. The group moves toward a circle of large stones. They wait for the sun to rise on the longest day of summer.

Soon Stonehenge is covered in light. The sun rests atop one of the stones. Everyone watches and wonders: "Who built this place? What was it for?"

WHAT IS STONEHENGE?

Stonehenge is an old **monument** in Wiltshire, England. It was built between about 3000 and 1500 BCE. The stones form a rough circle. They came from many miles away.

England

Wiltshire

N
W   E
S

sarsen stones

bluestones

Stonehenge began as a large circle carved in the earth. People later built a smaller circle of **bluestones** inside. Giant **sarsen stones** were placed around them.

Stonehenge is part of a larger **sacred** area. Graves have been found at the site. Also, the sun lines up with its stones on **solstices**. Still, no one knows for sure why it was built.

SURROUNDING STONEHENGE

Scientists use special tools to see beneath Stonehenge. They have found other monuments underground nearby.

STILL A MYSTERY

Many people think Stonehenge was used for **ceremonies**. Some have claimed it was a **temple** for **Druids**. A few think **aliens** helped people build it.

A MYSTERIOUS GROUP

The Druids were a group that lived in the area long ago. Little is known about their lives or beliefs.

Other people note that the stones sometimes align with the sun. They believe Stonehenge tracked the movements of the sun, moon, and stars.

SOUNDING STONES
Stonehenge may have been an early concert hall. The stones sound like bells when struck.

Another **theory** is that **festivals** were held at Stonehenge. It may also have been a place for healing. Some people believe it was mainly a burial site.

BUILDING STONEHENGE

3000-2935 BCE:

Builders carve out a ring and dig 56 holes to hold wood or stones.

2640-2480 BCE:

Bluestones and sarsen stones are placed in smaller circles inside the ring.

2470-2280 BCE:

A path is dug from Stonehenge to a nearby river.

2280-1520 BCE:

The bluestones are moved inside the sarsen stones and more holes are dug.

Science has not yet solved the mystery of Stonehenge. Will we ever uncover its past? Or will we always wonder what secrets these stones hold?

GLOSSARY

aliens—beings from another planet

bluestones—the small, blue-gray stones found inside Stonehenge; these bluestones are made of dolerite.

ceremonies—formal events that mark important occasions

Druids—members of an ancient British religion

festivals—big parties or celebrations

monument—a human-made structure that honors a person or event

sacred—very important or holy

sarsen stones—the large stones found in the outer circle and inner arc of Stonehenge; sarsen stones are made of sandstone.

solstices—the two times each year when the sun is farthest north or south of the equator; solstices are the longest and shortest days of the year.

temple—a place of worship

theory—an idea that explains something

TO LEARN MORE

At the Library

Henzel, Cynthia Kennedy. *Stonehenge*. Edina, Minn.: ABDO Pub. Co., 2011.

Manning, Mick. *The Secrets of Stonehenge*. London, U.K.: Frances Lincoln Children's Books, 2011.

McClellan, Ray. *Alien Abductions*. Minneapolis, Minn.: Bellwether Media, 2014.

On the Web

Learning more about Stonehenge is as easy as 1, 2, 3.

1. Go to www.factsurfer.com.

2. Enter "Stonehenge" into the search box.

3. Click the "Surf" button and you will see a list of related web sites.

With factsurfer.com, finding more information is just a click away.

INDEX